Verbs

Capture!

Run!

Hurry!

written by Ann Heinrichs

illustrated by Dan McGeehan and David Moore

The Child's World

Published by The Child's World®
1980 Lookout Drive • Mankato, MN 56003-1705
800-599-READ • www.childsworld.com

ACKNOWLEDGMENTS
The Child's World®: Mary Berendes, Publishing Director
The Design Lab: Design and page production
Red Line Editorial: Editorial direction

LIBRARY OF CONGRESS CATALOGING-IN-PUBLICATION DATA
Heinrichs, Ann.
 Verbs / by Ann Heinrichs ; illustrated by Dan McGeehan and David
Moore.
   p. cm.
 Includes bibliographical references and index.
 ISBN 978-1-60253-436-0 (library bound : alk. paper)
 1. English language—Verb—Juvenile literature. I. McGeehan, Dan, ill.
II. Moore, David, ill. III. Title.
 PE1271.H433 2010
 428.2—dc22   2010011462

Printed in the United States of America in Mankato, Minnesota.
November 2012
PA02156

ABOUT THE AUTHOR

Ann Heinrichs was lucky. Every year from grade three through grade eight, she had a big, fat grammar textbook and a grammar workbook. She feels that this prepared her for life. She is now the author of more than 100 books for children and young adults. She has also enjoyed successful careers as a children's book editor and an advertising copywriter. Ann grew up in Fort Smith, Arkansas, and lives in Chicago, Illinois.

ABOUT THE ILLUSTRATORS

Dan McGeehan spent his younger years as an actor, author, playwright, cartoonist, editor, and even as a casket maker. Now he spends his days drawing little monsters!

David Moore is an illustration instructor at a university who loves painting and flying airplanes. Watching his youngest daughter draw inspires David to illustrate children's books.

Giggle!

TABLE OF CONTENTS

What Is a Verb?

The kangaroo hopped over the fence.

Lauren feeds her turtle every day.

You eat too quickly!

Hopped, feeds, eat. These words are **verbs**. They show action.

Verbs are powerful words. They make things happen in a sentence. That's why every sentence must have a verb.

5

What's Happening Now?

Verbs can tell what's going on now, what happened long ago, or what's coming in the future.

Daniel leaves early on Fridays.

Jennifer loves checkers.

The planets orbit the sun.

Leaves, loves, orbit. These verbs show what is true right now. They are in the present **tense**. Other verb tenses show the past or the future.

What Happened Before?

The monster went home.

The cat chased the dog.

I lost my homework!

The past tense shows what happened before now. How do you make the past tense of a verb? You usually add *d* or *ed* to the present tense verb.

Present	Past
I climb trees.	I climbed trees last summer.
I help my mom.	I helped my mom last night.
I usually bathe the dog.	I bathed the dog this morning.

Break, Broke, Ring, Rang

Many verbs don't follow any rule for changing from present to past. You just have to know them by hearing and using them often. Luckily, you do!

Present	Past
break	broke
ring	rang
teach	taught
bring	brought

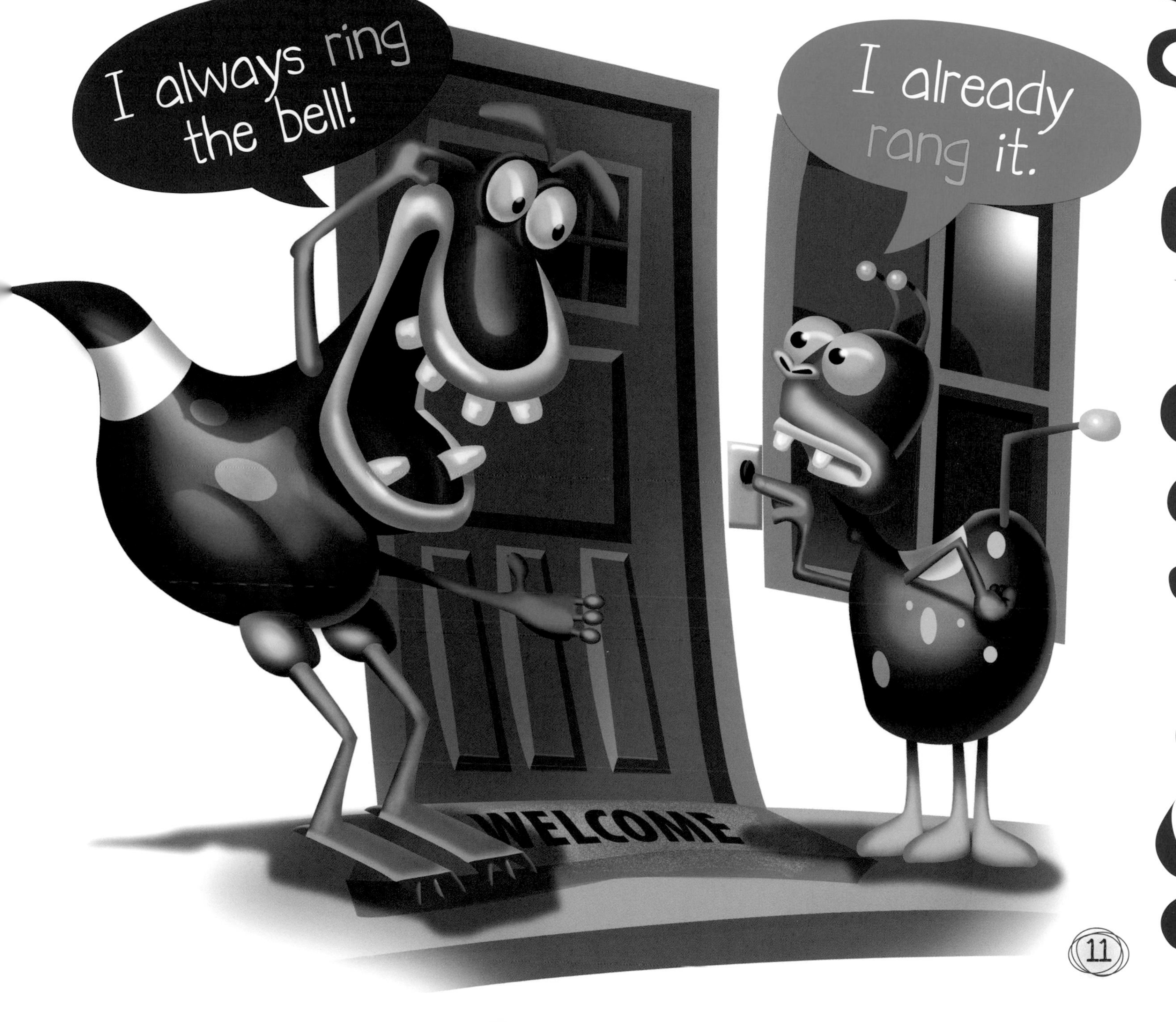
I always ring the bell!
I already rang it.
WELCOME

Is, Am, Are

I am very tall.

The monster is red.

They are happy.

Is, am, and are are three forms of the verb to be. This important verb does not show action. Instead, it helps describe things.

The witch is creepy.

The kids are scared of her.

Would you say "I is" or "She am"? Of course not. How do you know whether to choose is, am, or are? It depends on who is talking or what is being described.

Am	**Is**	**Are**
(for I)	*(for **singular** things)*	*(for **plural** things and you)*
I am sick.	The moon is full.	We are late.
	It is okay.	Monsters are noisy.
	He is wrong.	You are polite.
	She is happy.	We are late.
		They are bugging us.

Monsters are noisy!

To be has different forms for the past. Use was with *I* and other singular things, such as *the cat*. Use were with *you* and other plural things, such as *we* or *the monsters*.

Present	Past
I am cold.	I was cold last night.
The cat is sleepy.	The cat was sleepy this morning.
We are fast.	We were fast in the race yesterday.
You are silly.	You were silly at the party.
The monsters are hungry.	The monsters were hungry before breakfast.

15

Sometimes to be teams up with verbs that end in *ing*.

Dad is tickling Jim.
The clowns are making Tanya laugh!

The clowns didn't make Tanya laugh just once. You can tell from this verb form that Tanya keeps on laughing.

To be teams up with *ing* verbs in the past tense, too. It shows what was going on at a certain time.

I was taking a shower when the phone rang.

In the Future

It's easy to make the future tense. Just put will before any present-tense verb!

I will clean my room later.

Another way to make the future tense is to use to be plus going to and a present-tense verb.

I am going to clean my room later.

To be and other *ing* verbs tell what will be happening at a certain time in the future.

Sorry I can't come to your party.
I will be cleaning my room

Missing Letters

I'd   let's   you'll

These are **contractions**.

Saying *you'll* is shorter than saying *you will*. A contraction combines a verb with another word by leaving out letters. An **apostrophe** (') takes the place of the missing letters.

Full form	Contraction
I would	I'd
let us	let's
has not	hasn't
do not	don't
I am	I'm
you are	you're

Verbs can make a story more interesting and exciting. You might take a peek or tip-toe by, have a bite or chatter on. Can you think of more colorful ways to say look, walk, eat, and talk? What are some of your favorite action-packed verbs?

The next time someone tells a joke, don't just laugh. You could also chuckle, giggle, snicker, or howl.

How to Learn More

AT THE LIBRARY

Cleary, Brian P. *To Root, To Toot, To Parachute: What Is a Verb?*
Minneapolis, MN: Carolrhoda, 2001.

Fisher, Doris. *Home Run Verbs*. Pleasantville, NY: Gareth Stevens, 2008.

Fleming, Maria. *Verb for Herb*. New York: Scholastic, 2004.

Heller, Ruth. *Kites Sail High: A Book about Verbs*. New York: Putnam, 1988.

McClarnon, Marciann. *Painless Junior Grammar*. Hauppauge, NY:
Barron's Educational Series, 2007.

Reeg, Cynthia. *Doggy Day Camp: Verb and Adverb Adventures*. St. Louis,
MO: Guardian Angel Publishing, 2008.

Schoolhouse Rock: Grammar Classroom Edition. Dir. Tom Warburton.
Interactive DVD. Walt Disney, 2007.

ON THE WEB

Visit our home page for lots of links about grammar: *childsworld.com/links*

NOTE TO PARENTS, TEACHERS AND LIBRARIANS: We routinely check our Web links to make sure they're safe, active sites—so encourage your readers to check them out!

Glossary

apostrophe (uh-POSS-truh-fee): A punctuation mark that takes the place of the missing letters in a contraction. The apostrophe in *I'd* takes the place of the missing letters from *I would*.

contractions (kun-TRAK-shuns): Contractions are two words combined with some letters left out to make a shorter word. Contractions combine a verb with another word.

plural (PLOOR-uhl): A word is plural if it names more than one thing. *Monsters* and *we* are plural words.

singular (SING-gyuh-lur): A word is singular if it names one thing. *Monster* and *I* are singular words.

tense (TENSS): A form of a verb that shows when the action happened: in the present, the past, or the future. *Break* is a present tense verb and *broke* is a past tense verb.

verbs (VURBS): Action words that describe things to do or ways to be. *Run* and *help* are both verbs.

Index